E C O N O M I C   I S S U E S

24

Full Dollarization

The Pros and Cons

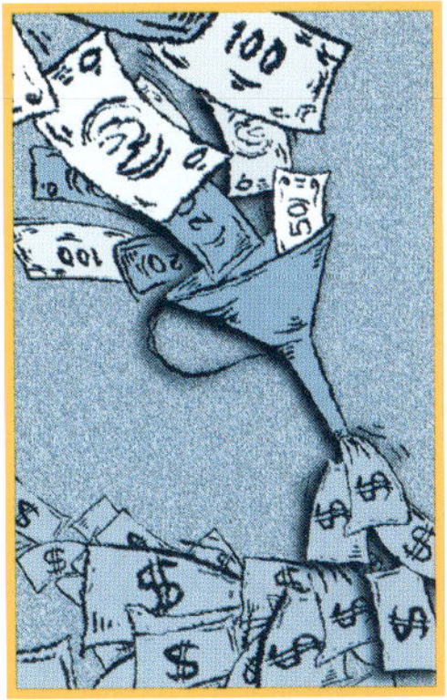

Andrew Berg
Eduardo Borensztein

INTERNATIONAL MONETARY FUND
WASHINGTON, D.C.

Series Editor
Jeremy Clift
IMF External Relations Department

Cover design and composition
Massoud Etemadi, Jack Federici, and
the IMF Graphics Section

ISBN 1-55775-993-6
ISSN 1020-5098

Published December 2000

To order IMF publications, please contact:

International Monetary Fund, Publication Services
700 19th Street, N.W., Washington, D.C. 20431, U.S.A.
Tel: (202) 623-7430 Telefax: (202) 623-7201
E-mail: publications@imf.org
Internet: http://www.imf.org

Preface

The Economic Issues Series aims to make available to a broad readership of nonspecialists some of the economic research being produced on topical issues by the International Monetary Fund. The series draws mainly from IMF Working Papers, technical papers produced by IMF staff members and visiting scholars, as well as from policy-related research papers.

The following paper draws on material originally contained in IMF Working Papers 00/50 and 00/29, respectively, "The Pros and Cons of Full Dollarization" and "The Choice of Exchange Rate Regime and Monetary Target in Highly Dollarized Economies," both by Andrew Berg and Eduardo Borensztein. Readers may purchase these papers for $10 each from IMF Publication Services. Charles S. Gardner prepared this version.

The Pros and Cons of Full Dollarization

Since the end of the Bretton Woods system of fixed exchange rates nearly thirty years ago, the old dilemma facing countries of finding workable currency exchange arrangements has become more challenging, and the choices have become more varied.

The decision about which exchange rate system to adopt has become more difficult as world trade and capital markets have become more integrated. New problems have emerged, and with them, new answers to the question of the best exchange regime to promote each country's development objectives. The newest of these solutions is full dollarization, under which a country officially abandons its own currency and adopts a more stable currency of another country—most commonly the U.S. dollar—as its legal tender.

From the perspective of any hard currency country, full dollarization may appear more radical than it is: use of the U. S. dollar or another major currency is pervasive to one degree or another in most developing countries, particularly in financial contracts (see Box 1, "What Is Dollarization?"). Full dollarization means taking the next step, from informal, limited dollarization to full, official use of the foreign currency in all transactions.

The main attraction of full dollarization is the elimination of the risk of a sudden, sharp devaluation of the country's exchange rate. This may allow the country to reduce the risk premium attached to its international borrowing. Dollarized economies could enjoy a higher level of confidence among international investors, lower interest rate spreads on their international borrowing, reduced fiscal costs, and more investment and growth.

Box 1. What Is Dollarization?

This pamphlet focuses on *full dollarization*, or one country officially adopting the currency of another for all financial transactions, except perhaps the need for coins. In considering this choice of exchange regime, two points are important to keep in mind:

- The term *dollarization* is shorthand for the use of any foreign currency by another country. The issues it raises are identical for the other countries in the region using the South African *rand*, for example, and they would be for any country of, say, Eastern Europe, considering eventually adopting the *euro*.
- Most developing countries—as well as transitional economies just adopting market mechanisms—already have a limited, unofficial form of dollarization. To a greater or lesser degree, their residents already hold foreign currency and foreign currency-denominated deposits at domestic banks. In high inflation countries, dollars or some other hard currency may be in widespread use in daily transactions, alongside the local currency.

Such informal dollarization is a response to economic instability and high inflation, and the desire of residents to diversify and protect their assets from the risks of devaluation of their own currencies. It is useful to distinguish between two motives for the demand for foreign currency assets: *currency substitution* and *asset substitution.*

In *currency substitution* foreign assets are used as money, essentially as means of payment and unit of account, and it typically arises under conditions of high inflation or hyperinflation when the high cost of

Questions About Pegs

Can these advantages offset the costs of a country giving up its own currency? The answers are complex, and in the end turn on each country's specific circumstances. But more and more countries are seriously considering full dollarization as they deal with the changes in the world economy, particularly over the past 20 years.

During the inflation-plagued 1980s, much of the debate over exchange regimes for developing countries centered on the role of exchange rate "pegs". Countries generally pick from a range of possibilities, including tying their currencies to baskets of other currencies (such as those of their trading partners), indexing their curren-

using domestic currency for transactions prompts the public to look for available alternatives. Once the use of foreign currency in transactions becomes accepted, it may not be rapidly abandoned. Remarkably, the increase in dollarization in some Latin American and Asian countries has continued and accelerated in recent years even following successful stabilization.

Asset substitution results from risk and return considerations about domestic and foreign assets. Historically, foreign currency-denominated assets have provided the opportunity of insuring against macroeconomic risks, such as price instability and prolonged depressions in many developing countries. Even under conditions of current stability, foreign currency-denominated assets may still serve this purpose if residents believe there is even a small chance of inflationary relapse.

Important differences exist between informal and full dollarization, presenting transitional problems for governments considering it. All government and private debt under full dollarization is denominated in dollars, and both public and private accounts must be converted to dollars. To make the conversion, countries must set the rate at which old debts, contracts, and financial assets will be converted to dollars.

Finally, the stability promised by dollarization is itself relative, given that the U.S. dollar—or any other hard currency chosen for use by another country—will fluctuate in value against other widely-traded currencies. During the post-Bretton Woods period, these swings have sometimes been large.

cies in some way to their own inflation rates, or even banding together in groups, as many French-speaking African nations have through currency unions tied to the French franc.

In the 1990s, global inflation abated and capital mobility and the scale of capital flows increased sharply. While countries welcomed the investment flows, they faced a new threat, as speculative attacks rose in frequency and severity against currencies that capital markets viewed as vulnerable to devaluation.

Generally, the victims of these currency crises were maintaining some sort of pegged exchange rate regime. Consequently, the belief began to emerge that in a world of high capital mobility, exchange rate pegs might themselves attract speculative attacks and that only extreme choices, such as a free float or a currency board were viable. The currency board regime, under which the domestic currency is fully backed by international reserves, is the strongest form of pegged exchange rate option.

Advocates of full dollarization attack both of these choices. Free floats, they argue, are not viable for many developing countries because they risk excessive exchange rate volatility. So far, only the largest developing economies, with relatively advanced financial systems, such as Korea, Brazil, and Mexico, have attempted floating. While experience is limited, these experiments have worked thus far without major disruption.

Meanwhile, currency boards have fallen prey to costly speculative attacks. Argentina and Hong Kong SAR[1], using currency boards successfully, nonetheless suffered sharp increases in interest rates and recessions in recent years as speculative attacks spread to them from other countries.

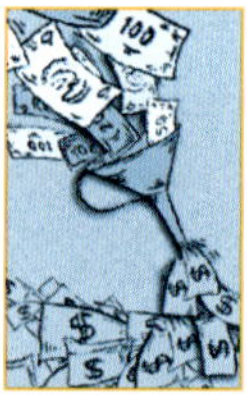

The Appeal of Dollarization

Against this background, then-president Carlos Menem of Argentina suggested in 1999 that Argentina adopt the U.S. dollar as the ultimate solution to its long history of difficulties with monetary and exchange rate policy. In January 2000, Ecuador, in the context of a deep economic and political crisis, adopted the U.S. dollar as its legal tender.

Prominent economists have begun to argue that essentially all developing countries should dollarize, and some industrial countries have even been urged to consider it. Partly prompted by the example of European countries giving up their currencies for the euro,

[1]Special Administrative Region of the People's Republic of China

some have suggested that Canada should adopt the U.S. dollar as the North American Free Trade Agreement (NAFTA) evolves.

Weighing the pros and cons of full dollarization is complicated by the virtual absence of historical experiences. Panama is the only sizable country with a history of using a foreign currency—the U. S. dollar—as legal tender, and it is fairly small, and has very close historical, political, and economic links to the United States. Even if there were more country experiences to assess, they would have to be over longer periods than is usual for evaluating monetary and exchange rate options. That is because dollarization is nearly permanent, and some of its benefits can be gained only in the long run.

This analysis of full dollarization compares it to its nearest competitor, the currency board. This comparison captures the main implications of dollarization and how its effects differ from those of simply adopting a very firm peg. Furthermore, if the costs and benefits of a currency board turn out to be at least equivalent to dollarization, a currency board would be a simpler and preferable alternative for a country seeking a firmly pegged exchange regime.

The differences between currency boards and dollarization are few, but important. Dollarization's key distinguishing feature is that it is permanent, or nearly so. Reversing dollarization is much more difficult than modifying or abandoning a currency board arrangement. In fact, the largest benefits claimed from dollarization derive from the credibility it carries precisely *because* it is nearly irreversible. And yet for some countries under particular circumstances, the irreversibility could come at a very high cost.

A government adopting full dollarization gives up the revenue from the loss of seigniorage (see Box 2, What Is Seigniorage?), whereas a currency board country does not. But a dollarizing country, by completely eliminating the risk of currency devaluation, gains lower interest rates on foreign borrowing.

The analysis below examines these issues in more detail. Quantifying the potential savings from lower interest rates turns out to be more complex than it first appears, but the cost of seigniorage loss can be roughly estimated. Important effects on economic stability and global financial integration resist quantification. Giving up any possibility of devaluation is costly for some countries, negligi-

Box 2. What Is Seigniorage?

The ancient concept of seigniorage as a government's profit from issuing coinage that costs less to mint than its face value is essentially the same with paper currencies: abstracting from the minor cost of printing paper money, seigniorage is simply the increase in the volume of domestic currency.

Currency can be thought of as non-interest bearing debt, and the ability to issue it as a source of revenue for the monetary authorities. In addition, reserve requirements on banks may also be non-interest bearing (or be remunerated well below market rates levels) and thus contribute to seigniorage. Thus, the annual flow of seigniorage is frequently measured as the increase in base money (the sum of currency plus bank reserves).

As counterpart of the issuance of currency, the central bank acquires assets that do pay interest, such as foreign currency reserves, government securities, and loans to private banks. In a currency board system, for example, the central bank must acquire foreign reserves in an amount equal to the domestic currency issue. As a result of issuing non-interest bearing debt (currency) and holding interest-earning assets (foreign reserves, etc.) the central bank earns a *gross* profit, which is often also called seigniorage by central banks.

ble for others. And all must consider the implications of a reduced national role in providing lender of last resort facilities and backing for their banking systems.

Is dollarization, then, a better exchange rate regime, especially for developing countries? The answer for each country depends ultimately on its own unique characteristics, but a closer look at the pros and cons of dollarization offers some general guidance.

The Risk Premium

An immediate benefit from eliminating the risk of devaluation is reducing the country risk premium on foreign borrowing and obtaining lower interest rates for the government and private investors. Lower interest rates and more stability in international capital movements cut the cost of servicing the public debt, and encourage higher investment and economic growth.

The magnitude of this potential gain is hard to measure. Argentina, now using a currency board under which the peso rate is fixed at a ratio of one-to-one to the U.S. dollar, provides a good example of the difficulties. There, a higher interest rate for borrowing in pesos than for U. S. dollars persists as evidence that lenders see a risk that the exchange rate peg will be abandoned. Yet interest rates on dollar-denominated Argentine government and private securities also exceed those on industrial countries' debt, reflecting a risk of default by the country, or sovereign risk, on those securities.

With dollarization, the interest premium owing to devaluation risk would disappear, but the premium for sovereign risk would not. Since government and the private sector can choose to borrow in foreign or domestic currency in Argentina's heavily dollarized economy, they can already eliminate the cost of devaluation risk by borrowing in dollars. The key question, then, is: would full dollarization, by eliminating currency risk, substantially reduce the default risk premium on dollar-denominated debt?

Examining yields on bonds with different features can help disentangle how markets perceive sovereign, or default, risk as distinct from devaluation risk. Sovereign risk can be measured by the spread on dollar-denominated Argentine government bonds over U. S. Treasuries. This spread has tended to come down with time, but has still averaged 3.3 percentage points during 1997–98. Devaluation risk can be measured by the spread between peso- and dollar-denominated Eurobonds, which averaged 2.5 percent over the same period.

Arguments exist on both sides of the question of how much of the sovereign, or default, risk to attribute to devaluation risk. Although sovereign risk and devaluation risk move closely together, this does not establish a causal link from one to the other. In fact, it is plausible that most of both dollar and peso spreads are explained by common factors. For example, a global "flight to quality" would raise both the measured risk of default and risk of devaluation. In this case, dollarization would not help reduce dollar spreads very much.

In fully dollarized Panama, for instance, the absence of currency risk does not insulate the country from swings in market sentiment toward emerging markets generally. Moreover, since movements in Panama's spreads cannot reflect devaluation risk, the implication is that at least a part of Argentina's spread also cannot be explained by currency risk alone.

Devaluation risk might increase sovereign risk for several reasons. For example, governments acting to avoid currency crises may be increasing the risk of default. Mexico did this in 1994 by issuing too many dollar-denominated bonds or dollar-indexed bonds in its defense of the peso. Or a government may impose capital controls, causing other debtors to default on dollar-denominated debt, as Russia did in 1998, blocking private debtors' access to foreign currency, and preventing them from servicing their foreign debt obligations. Conversely, devaluation may reduce default risk by improving the domestic economy and the fiscal position, as it has in the European Monetary System. Even devaluations that initially slow the economy may improve longer-term prospects and thus reduce the risk of sovereign default.

Only by analyzing historical interest rate data for individual countries is it possible to get a sense of the magnitude of the reduction in the risk premium in the event of dollarization, inferring what markets assess as the probability of default on foreign debt in the absence of currency crisis risk.

Seigniorage

A country adopting a foreign currency as legal tender sacrifices its seigniorage, the profits accruing to the monetary authority from its right to issue currency. The immediate cost of this issuance can be significant, and it continues on an annual basis thereafter.

Dollarization involves two kinds of seigniorage loss. The first is the immediate "stock" cost: as the dollar is introduced and the domestic currency withdrawn from circulation, the monetary authorities must buy back the stock of domestic currency held by the public and banks, effectively returning to them the seigniorage that had accrued over time. Second, the monetary authorities would give up future seigniorage earnings stemming from the flow of new currency printed every year to satisfy the increase in money demand.

In the case of Argentina, the first, or stock, cost of dollarization would be the redemption of about $15 billion in domestic currency held outside the central bank, or about 4.0 percent of gross domestic product (GDP). In addition, the loss of seigniorage on account of the increase in currency demand would amount to about another $1.0 billion annually, or about 0.3 percent of GDP.

For countries that do not already have enough foreign reserves to buy up their domestic currency and thereby dollarize, the acquisition of the initial stock could add indirect costs. If the country lacks the credit to borrow the reserves, it would be forced to accumulate them through current account surpluses. The cost of this could be substantial in forgone investment if, as is usual for developing countries, the better policy would otherwise be to run some sustainable level of current account deficit.

The United States would get more seigniorage from dollarization in other countries. There is, therefore, a case for the U.S. authorities to share part or all of these additional seigniorage revenues with countries that adopt the U. S. dollar. A precedent exists in the arrangements between South Africa and three other states that use the rand (Lesotho, Namibia, and Swaziland). While the United States has no sharing arrangement with Panama or any other legally dollarized economy, there have been some initiatives in the U.S. Senate to consider legislation providing for seigniorage reimbursement.

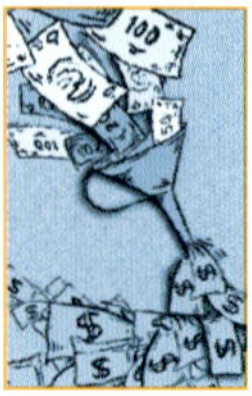

Stability

Important as risk spreads and seigniorage are, dollarization may offer gains that, although not immediately observable, may provide larger benefits over time. In addition to raising developing countries' borrowing costs, currency crises wreak havoc on the domestic economy. In Mexico, GDP fell by 7 percent in 1995, and the Asian countries affected by currency crises witnessed recessions in the range of 7–15 percent of GDP in 1998. Most of the severely affected countries in recent crises devalued and floated their exchange rate, but even countries with currency boards such as Hong Kong SAR and Argentina suffered fierce speculative attacks that, although weathered successfully, dealt them serious economic setbacks.

Dollarization will not eliminate the risk of external crises, since investors may flee because of problems of weakness in a country's budget position or the soundness of the financial system. This sort of "debt crisis" can be as damaging as any other, and indeed, Panama has experienced several.

Nevertheless, dollarization holds the promise of a steadier market sentiment as the elimination of exchange rate risk would tend to limit the incidence and magnitude of crisis and contagion episodes. Moreover, large swings in international capital flows cause sharp business cycle fluctuations in emerging economies even when they do not involve balance of payments crises.

Effect on Trade and Financial Links

A powerful but still longer-term argument for full, legal dollarization is that it makes economic integration easier with the rest of the world, and insulation of the domestic financial system correspondingly more difficult. Dollarization may establish a firm basis for a sound financial sector, and thus promote strong and steady economic growth. The argument here is that dollarization is perceived as an irreversible institutional change toward low inflation, fiscal responsibility, and transparency.

Furthermore, dollarization may contribute to greater economic integration than otherwise would be possible with the United States, or any other country whose currency is adopted. A number of studies have found evidence that Canadian provinces tend to be more integrated in trade volume and price level differences among themselves than with U.S. states that are closer geographically, trading in the order of twenty times more among themselves than with nearby U. S. states. The use of a common currency may thus be a vital factor in market integration, given the fairly low transaction costs and restrictions to trade across the U.S.-Canada border.

Dollarization could also bring about a closer integration in financial markets. One of the most profound effects of Panama's dollarization is the close integration of its banking system with that of the United States and indeed with the rest of the world, particularly since a major liberalization in 1969–70.

Exit Option

With full dollarization, a country completely gives up control of monetary and exchange rate policy. This may seem identical to currency board arrangements, since a country with a currency board cannot devalue. However, there is some scope for exit from the pegged exchange rate with a currency board, if only under extreme circumstances. Indeed, the elimination of this risk of devaluation is the main purpose of full dollarization.

Benefiting from Devaluation. Large shocks, such as a big jump in world oil prices or fall in the price of an important export, may require countries to devalue. Otherwise, they must absorb these shocks through lower nominal wages and adjustments in domestic prices. Substantial recession may then be unavoidable, particularly for economies with rigid labor markets.

Experiences such as departures from the gold standard and the 1994 devaluation of the CFA franc suggest that an exit option may have great value in the presence of extreme, unexpected shocks. During the Great Depression, for example, the industrial countries that fared best were those that exited earliest from the fixed exchange regime of the time—the gold standard. Argentina was one of them, suffering only a relatively minor economic setback by abandoning convertibility early, then actively stimulating the economy through monetary policy to offset the deflationary impact of capital outflows.

The countries of the CFA franc zone of West and Central Africa are recent examples of states with firmly pegged currencies that have successfully devalued to overcome severe external shocks and sluggish growth. The 14-nation franc zone resembles a currency board, with a fully convertible currency and an exchange rate fixed at par with the French franc from 1948 until 1994. From the second half of the 1980s into the early 1990s, output in the CFA franc zone stagnated as the French franc rose in value against the U.S. dollar, the CFA franc appreciated accordingly, the terms of trade deteriorated, and labor costs rose sharply. In 1994, the 14 countries resorted to a 50 percent devaluation, achieving a turnaround in higher output, exports, and investment.

Finally, countries with highly credible policymakers can also be well placed to benefit from devaluation, since the increase in expectations of inflation is likely to be lower than in countries with records of loose fiscal and monetary policies. For example, the CFA franc zone devaluation caused little inflation, occurring, as it did, against a long history of exclusive reliance on internal adjustments to deal with economic shocks.

Devaluations with High Cost. These examples suggest countries may pay a high price for foregoing the option to exit from a fixed exchange rate arrangement. The reverse is true where monetary policy has been poorly managed and expectations of inflation are highly sensitive to the exchange rate. In these countries, devaluation can sharply raise domestic prices, making it hard to achieve changes in the real exchange rate. Similarly, in countries that have become so dollarized that the dollar is often the de facto unit of account, devaluation quickly raises domestic prices, again limiting the effectiveness of devaluations. In fact, these were central reasons why Argentina adopted a currency board.

Countries with a high degree of financial asset dollarization have a further reason to avoid devaluation. If a country's banks or corporations receive large amounts of dollar-denominated lending, devaluation sharply worsens their balance sheets. Even if banks on-lend to domestic firms in dollars, maintaining matched risks in terms of currency on their books, they still carry a substantial currency risk. A sharp depreciation of the domestic currency would cause a large drop in revenues in dollar terms for the banks' clients, reducing their ability to service dollar debts.

As the currency crises in Mexico in 1994 and East Asia in 1997 demonstrated, when there are weak banking systems and large foreign exchange exposures in the private sector, the financial health of banks and firms is at such risk following a devaluation that economic activity is severely disrupted. Thus, devaluation as a policy option may be prohibitively costly for highly dollarized economies, and moving to full dollarization would not entail the loss of an important policy tool.

Lender of Last Resort Function and Financial System Stability

While full dollarization eliminates vulnerability of the banking system to the risk of devaluation, it does not eradicate all sources of banking crisis. And when they occur, full dollarization may well impair the country's lender-of-last-resort function and hence the central bank's response to financial system emergencies.

The central bank's role in operating a discount window to provide short-term liquidity must here be distinguished from its role as the ultimate guarantor of the stability of the financial and payments systems in the event of a systemic bank run. Dollarization should not greatly impede the ability of the authorities to provide short-term liquidity to the system or assistance to individual banks in distress. Such facilities are available if the central bank (or its replacement) saves the necessary funds in advance or perhaps secures lines of credit with international banks.

In contrast, the government loses some ability to respond to a sudden run on bank deposits throughout the entire system. In the case of a generalized loss of confidence, the authorities would be unable to guarantee the whole payments system or to fully back bank deposits. Ultimately, the ability to print money as needed is what allows a central bank to guarantee beyond any doubt that all claims (in domestic currency) will be fully met under any circumstances. Once the ability to print money ceases to exist, limits to the lender-of-last-resort function appear.A fully dollarized country that had already spent its foreign currency reserves to redeem its stock of domestic currency might well lack the resources to respond.

A Cushion for Currency Boards. Currency boards can create base money only to the extent that they accumulate reserves, so they are almost as tightly constrained as the monetary authorities would be in a dollarized economy. In important currency board cases, however, the authorities have allowed themselves some flexibility to create money that is not fully backed on the margin, partly to be able to deal with banking crises. In the case of the run on the Argentine peso during the 1995 "tequila" crisis, for example, the Argentine monetary authorities were able to partially accommodate the conversion of peso deposits into dollar deposits held abroad as well as into dollar cash.

By temporarily reducing their reserve coverage of the money base, they could increase the issuance of dollar cash and provide the dollar credits the banks needed to stay afloat. In the wake of the 1997 attack on the Hong Kong dollar, the Hong Kong Monetary Authority introduced in September 1998 a discount window to provide short-term liquidity to banks in a more flexible way and at lower cost than under previous arrangements. The new system is expected to reduce the volatility in short-term domestic interest rates. The maximum volume of rediscounts is limited, however, and the Hong Kong Monetary Authority fully backs rediscounts with foreign exchange.

The scope for accommodation to bank runs in a currency board is inevitably restricted. Indeed, even without the restrictions imposed by a currency board system, the ability of a central bank to find a way out of a financial crisis by resorting to printing money alone is limited. The injection of liquidity into the banking system to keep it from defaulting on deposits may only lead to greater pressure on foreign reserves or the exchange rate.

Conclusions

Summing up, the main pros and cons of dollarization are as follows:

Advantages

- Dollarization avoids currency and balance of payments crises. Without a domestic currency there is no possibility of a sharp depreciation, or of sudden capital outflows motivated by fears of devaluation.
- A closer integration with both the global and U. S. economies would follow from lower transaction costs and an assured stability of prices in dollar terms.
- By definitively rejecting the possibility of inflationary finance through dollarization, countries might also strengthen their financial institutions and create positive sentiment toward investment, both domestic and international.

Disadvantages

- Countries are likely to be reluctant to abandon their own currencies, symbols of their nationhood, particularly in favor of those of other nations. As a practical matter, political resistance is nearly certain, and likely to be strong.
- From an economic point of view, the right to issue a country's currency provides its government with seigniorage revenues, which show up as central bank profits and are transferred to the government. They would be lost to dollarizing countries and gained by the United States unless it agreed to share them.
- A dollarizing country would relinquish any possibility of having an autonomous monetary and exchange rate policy, including the use of central bank credit to provide liquidity support to its banking system in emergencies.

What is the balance of costs and benefits of full dollarization? The answers may seem frustratingly two-handed. This is inevitable, given the complexity of the issue and the current state of knowledge about it. The potential benefits of lower interest rates and the cost of forgone seigniorage revenues can at least be estimated. But many of the most important considerations, such as the value of keeping an exit option and lender of last resort protections, are virtually unquantifiable.

Which countries are likely to benefit from dollarization? The most obvious are those already highly integrated with the United States in trade and financial relations. Yet most countries in Latin America are quite different from the United States in their economic structure and would probably not benefit greatly from dollarization unless accompanied by deep market integration, as in the European Union.

The current discussion centers on a different group of candidates: emerging market economies exposed to volatile capital flows but not necessarily close, in an economic sense, to the United States. For this group, the more the U.S. dollar is already used in their domestic goods and financial markets, the smaller the advantage of keeping a national currency. For an economy that is already extremely dollarized, seigniorage revenues would be small (and the cost of purchasing the remaining stock of domestic currency also would be small), the exposures of banks and businesses would make devaluation financially risky, and the exchange rate would not serve as a policy instrument because prices would be "sticky" in dollar terms. In such cases, dollarization may offer more benefits than costs.

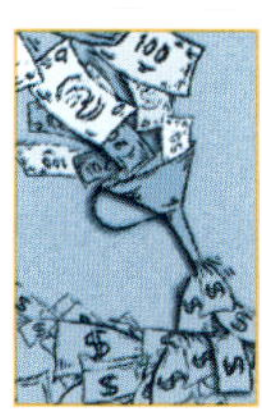

The full text of the original working paper, with supporting tables and graphs, can be found on the IMF website *http://www.imf.org/EXTERNAL/PUBS/CAT/shortres.cfm*

The Economic Issues Series

1. *Growth in East Asia: What We Can and What We Cannot Infer.* Michael Sarel. 1996.
2. *Does the Exchange Rate Regime Matter for Inflation and Growth?* Atish R. Ghosh, Anne-Marie Gulde, Jonathan D. Ostry, and Holger Wolf. 1996.
3. *Confronting Budget Deficits.* 1996.
4. *Fiscal Reforms That Work.* C. John McDermott and Robert F. Wescott. 1996.
5. *Transformations to Open Market Operations: Developing Economies and Emerging Markets.* Stephen H. Axilrod. 1996.
6. *Why Worry About Corruption?* Paolo Mauro. 1997.
7. *Sterilizing Capital Inflows.* Jang-Yung Lee. 1997.
8. *Why Is China Growing So Fast?* Zuliu Hu and Mohsin S. Khan. 1997.
9. *Protecting Bank Deposits.* Gillian G. Garcia. 1997.
10. *Deindustrialization—Its Causes and Implications.* Robert Rowthorn and Ramana Ramaswamy. 1997.
11. *Does Globalization Lower Wages and Export Jobs?* Matthew J. Slaughter and Phillip Swagel. 1997.
12. *Roads to Nowhere: How Corruption in Public Investment Hurts Growth.* Vito Tanzi and Hamid Davoodi. 1998.
13. *Fixed or Flexible? Getting the Exchange Rate Right in the 1990s.* Francesco Caramazza and Jahangir Aziz. 1998.
14. *Lessons from Systemic Bank Restructuring.* Claudia Dziobek and Ceyla Pazarbaşıoğlu. 1998.
15. *Inflation Targeting as a Framework for Monetary Policy.* Guy Debelle, Paul Masson, Miguel Savastano, and Sunil Sharma. 1998.
16. *Should Equity Be a Goal of Economic Policy?* IMF Fiscal Affairs Department. 1998.

17. *Liberalizing Capital Movements: Some Analytical Issues.* Barry Eichengreen, Michael Mussa, Giovanni Dell'Ariccia, Enrica Detragiache, Gian Maria Milesi-Ferretti, and Andrew Tweedie. 1999.

18. *Privatization in Transition Countries: Lessons of the First Decade.* Oleh Havrylyshyn and Donal McGettigan. 1999.

19. *Hedge Funds: What Do We Really Know?* Barry Eichengreen and Donald Mathieson. 1999.

20. *Job Creation: Why Some Countries Do Better.* Pietro Garibaldi and Paolo Mauro. 2000.

21. *Improving Governance and Fighting Corruption in the Baltic and CIS Countries: The Role of the IMF.* Thomas Wolf and Emine Gürgen. 2000.

22. *The Challenge of Predicting Economic Crises.* Andrew Berg and Catherine Pattillo. 2000.

23. *Promoting Growth in Sub-Saharan Africa: Learning What Works.* Anupam Basu, Evangelos A. Calamitsis, and Dhaneshwar Ghura. 2000.

24. *Full Dollarization: The Pros and Cons.* Andrew Berg and Eduardo Borensztein. 2000.